Read-About® Geography

Washington

By Susan Labella

Subject Consultant
Nancy B. Hultquist
Professor of Geography
Central Washington University, Ellensburg, Washington

Reading Consultant
Cecilia Minden-Cupp, PhD
Former Director of the Language and Literacy Program
Harvard Graduate School of Education
Cambridge, Massachusetts

Children's Press®
A Division of Scholastic Inc.
New York   Toronto   London   Auckland   Sydney
Mexico City   New Delhi   Hong Kong
Danbury, Connecticut

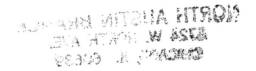

Designer: Herman Adler Design
Photo Researcher: Caroline Anderson
The photo on the cover shows wildflower meadows and Mount Rainier.

Library of Congress Cataloging-in-Publication Data

Labella, Susan, 1948–
  Washington / by Susan Labella.
    p. cm. — (Rookie Read-About Geography)
  Includes index.
  ISBN 0-516-24993-2 (lib. bdg.)   0-516-26455-9 (pbk.)
  1. Washington (State)—Juvenile literature. 2. Washington (State)—
Geography—Juvenile literature. I. Title. II. Series.
  F891.3.L35 2006
  917.97'02—dc22   2005021637

CHILDREN'S PRESS, and ROOKIE READ-ABOUT®,
and associated logos are trademarks and/or registered trademarks
of Scholastic Library Publishing. SCHOLASTIC and associated logos
are trademarks and/or registered trademarks of Scholastic Inc.
1 2 3 4 5 6 7 8 9 10 R 15 14 13 12 11 10 09 08 07 06

Which state is the Evergreen State?

3

It's Washington!

Washington is in the northwestern part of the United States.

Can you find Washington on this map?

CANADA

WASHINGTON

OREGON

MONTANA

NORTH DAKOTA

MINNESOTA

NEW HAMPSHIRE

VERMONT

MAINE

IDAHO

SOUTH DAKOTA

WISCONSIN

MICHIGAN

NEW YORK

MASSACHUSETTS

WYOMING

NEVADA

UTAH

NEBRASKA

IOWA

OHIO

PENNSYLVANIA

RHODE ISLAND

CONNECTICUT

NEW JERSEY

COLORADO

KANSAS

ILLINOIS

INDIANA

WEST VIRGINIA

DELAWARE

MARYLAND

CALIFORNIA

MISSOURI

KENTUCKY

VIRGINIA

Washington, D.C.

ARIZONA

NEW MEXICO

OKLAHOMA

ARKANSAS

TENNESSEE

NORTH CAROLINA

SOUTH CAROLINA

TEXAS

ALABAMA

MISSISSIPPI

GEORGIA

North

LOUISIANA

FLORIDA

West

East

South

ALASKA

CANADA

MEXICO

HAWAII

5

6

Forests cover about half
of Washington's land.
Fir, pine, spruce, and
cedar are just a few types
of trees that grow in
Washington's forests.

Washington's state tree is
the western hemlock.

Some trees are cut and trimmed into logs. These logs are cut into lumber. People use lumber to build houses and other items.

Washington's Olympic National Park has a temperate rain forest. A temperate rain forest is a wet place where trees, ferns, and other plants grow.

Visitors might see golden
beetles, cougars, black
bears, and elk there.

The Columbia River
flows through Washington.

Many dams have been built
on this river, including the
Grand Coulee Dam. This
large dam helps make
electricity for many homes
and businesses.

Washington has a lot of large
mountains. Many are good
for skiing and snowboarding.

Mount Rainier is Washington's highest point. It is a volcano.

Washington has beaches, too! Long Beach Peninsula has 28 miles (45 kilometers) of sandy beach.

Each year, a big kite festival takes place there.

Almost half of the apples grown in the United States come from Washington.

The apple is Washington's state fruit.

In spring, the apple trees bloom with beautiful white and pink flowers. These flowers are called blossoms.

Many people visit Wenatchee for the Apple Blossom Festival.

A lot of other flowers
bloom in Washington.

Washington's state flower
is the coast rhododendron.

Washington also has busy cities. Seattle is the largest city. It's home to a tall building called the Space Needle. The Space Needle stands 600 feet (183 meters) high.

Washington's capital
is Olympia.

Washington is the
20th-largest state in the
United States.

Maybe one day you will visit Washington.

What will you do when you get there?

Words You Know

apple

coast rhododendron

Grand Coulee Dam